THE WU STYLE OF
TAI CHI CHUAN

BY TINN CHAN LEE

太極拳

李天贊編著與示範

DEDICATION

To the memory of my father and mother, the late Mr. and Mrs. Lee Wai, who inspired me to study Tai Chi Ch'uan; to the United States of America, my adopted country; to my fellow Americans; and to all mankind.

© **UNIQUE PUBLICATIONS, INC., 1982**
All rights reserved
Printed in the United States of America
Library of Congress No.: 81-50511
ISBN: 0-86568-022-1

UNIQUE PUBLICATIONS

4201 VANOWEN PLACE, BURBANK, CA 91505

DISCLAIMER

Please note that the publisher of this instructional book is NOT RESPONSIBLE in any manner whatsoever for any injury which may occur by reading and/or following the instructions herein.

It is essential that before following any of the activities, physical or otherwise, herein described, the reader or readers should first consult his or her physician for advice on whether or not the reader or readers should embark on the physical activity described herein. Since the physical activities described herein may be too sophisticated in nature, *it is essential that a physician be consulted.*

ACKNOWLEDGEMENTS

I would like to thank Mr. Hee Yee for taking all the photographs. I would like to thank Dr. Robert Santee for helping me compile and edit this book and also for doing most of the typing.

TABLE OF CONTENTS

FOREWORD

T'ai Chi Ch'uan is an ancient Chinese art of self-defense. In the old days only noblemen could learn the art; it has been practiced in China for one thousand years.

Primarily, it is a philosophy of physical, mental and spiritual dimensions, based on the teachings of Lao Tzu of the Chou Dynasty, and was first developed by a Taoist saint.

It is a system of meditative exercise which prevents and heals ailments through revitalizing and rejuvenating the vital organs of the body if practiced regularly and accurately.

It is a series of continuous rhythmic steps that give the body healthful and harmonious movement. It is a nonstop slow exercise which takes twenty minutes or longer to perform. In fact, the slower the performance, the greater the benefits are.

The important principle of the art is relaxation, which encourages meditation. T'ai Chi Ch'uan encourages meditation in motion while it circulates the life fluid through the body. It is conducive to longevity. There are documentary evidences that some practitioners of this art have lived to a very old age.

The author of this book, Mr. Tinn Chan Lee, is a teacher of great experience, and an unassuming gentleman. Sickly as a young man, he took up T'ai Chi Ch'uan thirty-three years ago, first under Master Liu and then, in 1937, under Master Wu in Hong Kong. This great art has not only restored him to excellent health and youthful vigor, but has also given him a tranquillity of mind and spirit in a world where men constantly live under tremendous stresses of life.

Tien-Tse Chang, M.A., PhD., Litt.D. (Leiden)
Professor and Senior Specialist, East-West Center,
University of Hawaii, 1966.

PREFACE

When I was a young boy, I was weak and sickly. I asked my uncle to teach me the external style of Kung Fu. It did not help my weak condition; in fact, Kung Fu made me weaker because it took too much of my energy. I asked my father what to do and he suggested that I change to an internal style of Kung Fu like Tai Chi Ch'uan. The only problem with this was that a good teacher was hard to find. Since the internal style of Kung Fu is so complex and comprehensive, you must find a qualified teacher or you will end up on the wrong path.

After having studied and practiced Tai Chi Ch'uan for so many years, I have realized that I know very little about the depths of this great art. However, my mental and physical health have improved and I have achieved an inner peace.

Since Tai Chi Ch'uan has benefited me throughout my life, I would like to pass on my limited knowledge to my fellow Americans and also to those who are interested in the internal style of Kung Fu.

Tinn Chan Lee

MY GRACIOUS TEACHER, THE LATE WU KAM CHIN

香 港
鑑泉太極拳社簡章

香港鑑泉太極拳社簡章

第一條　本社為傳習太極拳藉以宣揚國術提倡體育聯絡友誼為宗旨

第二條　本社定名香港鑑泉太極拳社

第三條　本社址暫設灣仔軒鯉詩道二四一號於必要時得增設分社以便利社員就近練習

第四條　本社組織如左

甲　名譽社長若干人

乙　正社長一人副社長二人總理本社一切事務

丙　設聘請幹事若干人輔助正副社長掌理社務

丁　總務幹事掌教務交際宣傳會計庶務事宜

戊　設研究班普通班兒童班婦女班別或有相當之程度者得入研究

第五條　本社設幹事研究班研習於太極拳曾練習三年以上或學未學均可報名參加

第六條　本社分班有

甲　凡幹事為注重健身起見特聘兒童班及小學生曾練習太極拳者得入普通班練習

乙　凡學習或初學者得入普通班練習

丙　本社設兒童班婦女班教員一人擔任婦女班教授

丁　本社為便利兒童起見特設兒童班以資普及小學生均可來本社練習學費半價

戊　每日早七時至九時晚七時至九時男女童十五歲以上男女學生均為授課時間

第七條　本社經費如左

（五）本社名譽社長董事長每年特別捐助本社基金五百元或捐募

（四）本社名譽社董贊助社員每年贊助本社基金一百元

（三）本社社董贊助社員二人每年贊助費五十元

（二）本社基本社員每年繳納會費拾陸圓半年繳費捌圓式拾肆圓為基本社員

（一）本社太極拳教授社員隨時來社指導社董家屬及社員一外社員免費練習

第八條　本社社員介紹社員入社免收社費

第九條　本社贊助社員之子侄一人免費練習

第十條　本社社員學費徵求期介紹社員五人以上者則可免繳社費以所介紹

第十一條　本社凡練習時期限另表規定之

第十二條　本社各班課目進度另表規定之

第十三條　本社團體練習交通費另議之

第十四條　公本社各條規則及各班課目團體練習交通費另議定之

香港鑑泉太極拳社社員入社志願書

姓名	李天贄	籍貫	廣東出	性別	男	年齡	廿六
職業	檀山華僑	住址	基利支街日益隆金山庄				

敬啟者：茲願依照

貴社簡章之規定加入為社員，凡社中一切規章，及決議案，皆願遵守，即希登記准予入社，為荷此上

香港鑑泉太極拳社

請求入社人　李天贄　印

介紹人　梁志榮　印

中華民國廿六　年　月　日

社　長　吳鑑泉
副社長　唐希文　謹訂
　　　　鄭榮光

APPLICATION TO THE SCHOOL OF WU KAM CHIN

CHAPTER 1

INTRODUCTION

Tai Chi Ch'uan is the ancient Chinese art and science of meditation through movement. It is based on the philosophical and mystical teachings of both the *I Ching* and China's great sage, Lao Tzu. Tai Chi Ch'uan reflects ancient observations of the Yin (negative) and Yang (positive) principles in nature.

Unlike Indian Yoga, which is based on individual and static postures, Tai Chi Ch'uan consists of unbroken rhythmic movements that flow with complete relaxation. This flowing relaxation benefits the entire body simultaneously. Through proper breath control and concentration, this flowing relaxation will result in complete mental control, physical and emotional well-being and inner peace. To achieve these benefits, however, Tai Chi Ch'uan must be studied under a qualified teacher and practiced consistently for an extended period of time.

Considering the stress under which most people live in modern civilization, this ancient wisdom from China is of utmost importance for present day man. Tai Chi Ch'uan is a form of effortless, gradual and continuous movement which harmonizes with nature and the universe. If properly performed, it revives, revitalizes and, in time, after long practice, rejuvenates every cell of the human body. Thus, it is possible to restore a sick body or improper mental attitude to perfect health again.

There is an esoteric as well as an exoteric side to Tai Chi Ch'uan and the former is by far more important than the latter, which is only an outer expression of the core of Tai Chi Ch'uan. Tai Chi Ch'uan is spiritual release and emancipation through meditation in motion. There are five orders or steps to be accomplished:

1. Transforming the physical body through motion to generate more life fluid.
2. Transforming the life fluid into circulating breath. This is not the breath from ordinary exercise which inflates and deflates the lungs, but the primary breath, which is created and generated in the lower psychic center, that moves through the body in harmony with sustained rhythm.
3. Combining life fluid and circulating breath with life spirit.
4. Transforming the life spirit into the Void. At this stage, Tai Chi Ch'uan is moving into the spiritual dimension.
5. Transforming the Void into the Tao.

Prior to the first step, there are ten fundamental principles that govern the movements of Tai Chi Ch'uan. They are:

1. The upper psychic center (the top of the head) is made as light (yin) as possible. The lower psychic center (1 to 2 inches below the navel) is made as heavy (yang) as possible.
2. Use the mental process. Do not use physical strength.
3. The chest is not expanded nor pushed forward. The back is slightly curved.

4. Sink the shoulders and lower the elbows.
5. The spine and sacrum must be straight. All movement originates from the pivoting of the sacrum.
6. The upper and lower body are in perfect coordination.
7. The inner and the outer harmonies are synchronized.
8. Polarize the body and its movements. The yin and yang aspects are clearly distinguished.
9. Create elastic-like movements in an unbroken sequence. The body is always rotating.
10. Within movement seek tranquillity. Tranquillity and movement are harmonized into one.

The ten important rules that govern the movements of Tai Chi Ch'uan.

The upper psychic center is made as light (yin) as possible. The lower psychic center is made as heavy (yang) as possible.

Use the mental process. Do not use physical strength.

The chest is not expanded nor pushed forward. The back is slightly curved. Sink the shoulders and lower the elbows.

Polarize the body and its movements. The yin and yang aspects are clearly distinguished.

The spine and sacrum must be straight. All movements originate from the pivoting of the sacrum.

The upper body and the lower body are in perfect coordination.

The inner and outer harmonies are synchronized.

Create elastic-like movements in an unbroken sequence. The body is always rotating.

Within movements seek tranquility. Tranquility and movements are harmonized into one.

AN EXPLANATION OF THE
TEN FUNDAMENTAL PRINCIPLES

1. *The upper psychic center is made as light as possible. The lower psychic center is made as heavy as possible.*
This procedure is created by the use of the mind. The mind imagines the upper psychic center to be light and the lower psychic center to be heavy. The result of the movement of the mind and the correct body position is relaxation. When there is relaxation the Ch'i will sink down to the lower psychic center. The body must be held straight and there can be no use of physical strength.

2. *Use the mental process. Do not use physical strength.*
If physical strength is used the Ch'i will not circulate. Physical strength prevents the flow of Ch'i through the body. Ch'i will only flow when the body is relaxed and the mind is in control. The mind directs the flow of Ch'i.

3. *The chest is not expanded nor pushed forward. The back is slightly curved.*
If the chest is expanded the Ch'i will rise up. If the back is too straight the Ch'i will not sink down. If the Ch'i rises up and is unable to sink down, then the center of balance will rise up.

4. *Sink the shoulders and lower the elbows.*
If the shoulders are not down the Ch'i will not sink, the body will not be relaxed and the center of balance will rise up. This is also true if the elbows are not lowered.

5. *The spine and sacrum must be straight. All movement originates from the pivoting of the sacrum.*
If the body is not aligned the Ch'i will not sink down and there will be no relaxation. If the movements are not from the sacrum the Ch'i will not circulate harmoniously.

6. *The upper and lower body are in perfect coordination.*
The shoulders are in line with the hips. The knees are in line with the elbows. The top of the head is in line with the base of the spine. These three alignments are called the three outer harmonies.

7. *The inner and the outer harmonies are synchronized.*
The three outer harmonies must be in a rhythmic flow with the three inner harmonies. The three inner harmonies are: The life fluid is in harmony with the life spirit; the life spirit is in harmony with the circulating breath; the circulating breath is in harmony with the life fluid. The inner and the outer aspects of man must flow as one.

8. *Polarize the body and its movements. The yin and yang aspects are clearly distinguished.*

The forward movements are in harmony with the backward movements. The movements to the right are in harmony with the movements to the left. The movements of the hands are in harmony with the movements of the feet. The upper body is in harmony with the lower body. The body must always manifest both yin and yang aspects.

9. *Create elastic-like movements in an unbroken sequence. The body is always rotating.*

Each movement blends into the next movement. The body is in continuous motion with no stopping. All motion is circular.

10. *Within movement seek tranquillity. Tranquillity and movement are harmonized into one.*

Within the activity of movement there is tranquillity. When tranquillity is found it must be harmonized with movement. This is Tai Chi meditation.

The esoteric aspect of Tai Chi development.
Steps leading to the Secret of the Golden Flower.

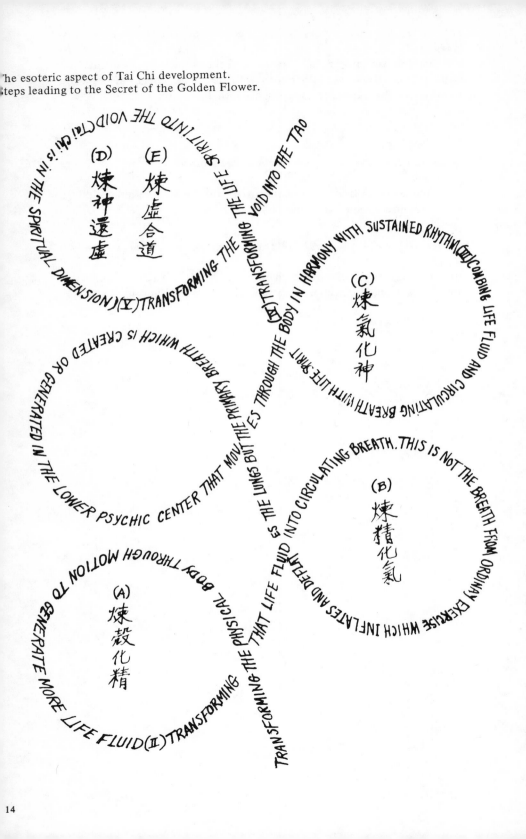

A BRIEF HISTORY OF THE TAI CHI CH'UAN MASTERS

According to some authorities on Tai Chi Ch'uan, the original master was Chang San Feng. He was a scholar, during the Soong dynasty, who mastered the martial art of self-defense in its external style and later developed the internal style known as Tai Chi Ch'uan.

Until the time of Chang San Feng, Tai Chi Ch'uan was probably a series of individual static postures. It is believed that Chang San Feng was responsible for perfecting Tai Chi Ch'uan by putting the postures into a form of continuous and rhythmic movements which are regulated by breath control.

Actually, Chang San Feng should not be considered the founder of Tai Chi Ch'uan, but the developer of the style that is practiced in its present form. His conceptions about the structure of Tai Chi Ch'uan are based on the theory of the Eight Trigrams from the *I Ching,* the teachings of the *Tao Te Ching* and probably the *Washing the Marrow* and the *Changing the Sinews* attributed to Bodhidharma. Within this structure, he incorporated a system of deep and controlled breathing.

Other writers on Tai Chi Ch'uan believe that the origin dates back to the Leong dynasty and was actually founded by Ching Ling Sin. This style was not, however, perfected as it is today. Ching Ling Sin handed down his teachings to his disciple, Han Koong Yit, who transmitted these teachings to his own disciple, Ching Be. During this period, Tai Chi Ch'uan was known as Siu Kow Tin or literally "The Small Nine Heavens."

During the Tang dynasty there lived the master Lee Tao Tze. He created his own system of Tai Chi Ch'uan called "Sin Tin Kin" or the "Primeval Art of Shadow Boxing." He transmitted his teachings to his disciples Yee Ching Wai, Yee Yat Seung and Yee Lin Chow.

Another great master was Hoo (Hu) Kang Tze. He handed down his knowledge to his disciple, the poet and scholar Soong Jung Chi. He called his style by the name of "Ho Tin Fa" or the "Secondary Art of Shadow Boxing." He handed down his teachings to Yun Lee Hing.

Now we come, once again, to Chang San Feng. When he was a young child he showed a remarkable ability in several areas. As a young man he was recognized as a scholar in literature. He passed the highest civil service exams for his area and was made a government official. He was indifferent toward his government post because he was not interested in personal power or glory. He was interested, instead, in the meditative life. Finally, he resigned from his government post and retired to an isolated mountain retreat on Wu Tang Mountain.

According to legend, one day Chang San Feng, while meditating at his mountain retreat, saw a battle between a snake and a white crane. Observing their natural and skillful movements, he conceived the idea of the internal, flowing form of Tai Chi Ch'uan. With a young companion, he practiced Tai Chi Ch'uan meditation for a long period of time. At the age of 67, seeking for further knowledge in the Tao, he went to another mountain range called Chung Nam. There he met a great Ch'an (Zen) master called For Loong Jun

Yun, the "Holy Fire Dragon Man." It was through his teachings that Chang San Feng became enlightened. He later took two other names and was known as Hin Hin Tze and as Kwun Young Jun Yun. He transmitted his teachings to his disciple Wong Chung Ngok. This gifted disciple methodically explained and formalized all the important basic principles and treaties of Tai Chi Ch'uan that we use today.

He handed this down to his disciple Chun Chow Toong in the district of Wan Chow in central China. His teachings are usually referred to as the Southern Style. The Wan Chow branch of Tai Chi Ch'uan produced the noted master Cheong Chung Kai.

The style of Chiang Fat of Honan province in northern China is usually referred to as the Northern Style. Chiang Fat transmitted his teachings to his disciple Chun Cheong Hing and he, in turn, handed down these teachings to his disciple Yang Loo Sim. Yang Loo Sim was a very methodical and enthusiastic teacher of this art. He was very prominent in Peking during the Ching dynasty and members of the ruling class studied under him. In those days, Tai Chi Ch'uan was taught almost exclusively to the aristocracy and to wealthy families.

Yang Loo Sim had three sons. The first born son passed away at an early age. The second son was named Yang Barn Ho, while the third son was named Yang Kin Ho. They were both prominent teachers of Tai Chi Ch'uan. Yang Kin Ho had three sons who were also very famous teachers of Tai Chi Ch'uan. The second son passed away at an early age. The eldest son was named Yang Siu Ho, while the youngest son was named Yang Ching Hoo.

When Yang Loo Sim lived in Peking, there were only three disciples who received the esoteric side of his teachings. They were Wu Chin Yow, Marn Chun and Ling San. It was Wu Chin Yow who developed the Wu style of Tai Chi Ch'uan. Wu Chin Yow transmitted these teachings to his only son, Wu Kam Chin. Wu Kam Chin was the teacher of many disciples all over China. Wu Kam Chin had two sons. They were named Wu Kung Yee and Wu Kung Chow. They both received their father's teachings and passed them on to their own disciples.

The Southern style of Tai Chi Ch'uan declined over a period of time and it was the Northern style, operating in a more vigorous climate and with a greater cultural past, that spread and survived till this day.

PHILOSOPHICAL FOUNDATIONS

The philosophical basis of Tai Chi Ch'uan can be found in the *I Ching* and the *Tao Te Ching*. The two basic principles of Tai Chi Ch'uan can be found in the following quotes:

By attending to Ch'i and relaxing completely, you will be able to be like a new born babe.
Tao Te Ching
Chapter 10

Yin and Yang in succession is called Tao.
I Ching
Ta Chuan

The concern of Tai Chi Ch'uan is with the cultivation of *Ch'i*. This is accomplished through relaxation and breath control. Through this process the entire body is revitalized and the individual is, thus, born anew. He is like a newborn babe. But Tai Chi Ch'uan is not merely concerned with the revitalization of the individual's body, but with his spiritual development and enlightenment. If man is able to flow from positive to negative and from negative to positive, he will be in harmony with the universe. To be in harmony with the universe is Yin and Yang in succession. Yin and Yang in succession is called Tao. It is the goal of the student of Tai Chi Ch'uan to become one with the Tao.

The formal exercise of Tai Chi Ch'uan is a flowing process that moves through a positive and negative series. As life is a continual flow so is Tai Chi Ch'uan a continual flow. The body is guided through the form of Tai Chi Ch'uan by the flow of the mind and the flow of *Ch'i*. This entire process is meditation in motion. Through this meditation the student will achieve enlightenment.

CHAPTER 2

THE SEVEN BASIC STANCES

There are seven fundamental stances in Tai Chi Ch'uan. They are the Parallel Stance, the Sitting Stance, the Bow Stance, the Horse Stance, the Treading Stance, the Half-Split Leg Stance, and the Single Foot Stance. The second, third and fourth stances can be practiced independently as static meditative exercises which will be described later.

These meditative exercises are concerned with the cultivation of internal energy. The Chinese call this internal energy *Ch'i*. The static meditative exercises to develop this *Ch'i* are not to be attempted by the beginning student. Only after the student has performed the formal exercises of Tai Chi Ch'uan for a few years should he attempt to perform the static meditative exercises. If the body is not conditioned through the formal exercises of Tai Chi Ch'uan, and the student attempts to perform the static meditative exercises prematurely, he will tend to develop awkward, angular movements rather than smooth, circular movements. Smooth circular movements will facilitate the flow of *Ch'i* throughout the body.

Each of the three stances have different functions so that they allow the student to cultivate *Ch'i*. The stances are concerned with the development of balance, posture, concentration, breathing, proper footwork, the alignment of the internal organs and the alignment of the three psychic centers. The three psychic centers are the upper Tan T'ien (top of the head), the middle Tan T'ien (solar plexus) and the lower Tan T'ien (one to two inches below the navel).

It is necessary to follow the descriptions of the stances exactly because *Ch'i* can only flow when everything is in proper alignment. When everything is in proper alignment, then the body is completely relaxed. When the body is relaxed, then *Ch'i* will sink down to the lower Tan T'ien. It is from the lower Tan T'ien that *Ch'i* will then flow throughout the rest of the body. As the student advances in the cultivation of *Ch'i*, there will be a point where he will be able to direct *Ch'i* to any point in his body.

The level of attainment, however, is dependent upon the student's ability to align his body both within and without. It is only through relaxation that *Ch'i* will sink down to the lower Tan T'ien. This is a long process and requires the use of the mind to assist in the cultivation. The final goal is to send *Ch'i* throughout the body under the control of the mind.

PRINCIPLES FOR THE CULTIVATION
OF CH'I

1. The body is held straight.
2. Everything is completely relaxed.
3. The mind imagines *Ch'i* sinking down to the lower Tan T'ien.
4. The tongue touches the roof of the mouth.
5. Control the breathing through the use of the diaphragm. Inhale through the nose and exhale through the mouth for the first three breaths. All subsequent breathing is performed only through the nose. When inhaling the abdomen must expand. When exhaling the abdomen contracts. The breathing process must be deep, relaxed, slow and controlled every inch of the way.

DURATION OF THE STATIC MEDITATIVE
EXERCISES

As mentioned previously there are three static meditative stances—the Sitting Stance, the Bow Stance, and the Horse Stance. Begin by holding each of the static meditative stances for about five minutes. Gradually work up to ten minutes for each stance. This can be accomplished by adding one to two minutes a week for each of the stances. The goal is to perform each of the stances for twenty or more minutes. As one progresses in the performance of each stance, it would probably be more beneficial to perform only one or two stances a day. The ultimate goal is not an endurance record. The ultimate goal is the cultivation of *Ch'i*.

THE PARALLEL STANCE

Stand straight with the feet shoulder width apart. The body weight is equally distributed. The head is held straight while the eyes are looking forward. The knees are slightly bent. The hands are held at chest level with the fingers pointing up and the palms pointing forward. The hands are held about ten to twelve inches in front of the body with the elbows pointing down. The arms are held away from the body at a distance of the size of one fist. There can be no tension. The body is completely relaxed from the top of the head down to the toes.

THE SITTING STANCE

The right leg is forward and rests on the heel of the right foot. The left leg is to the rear and is slightly bent. All the body weight is on the rear foot. The arms are held in front of the body and are slightly rounded with the elbows pointing straight down. The palm of the right hand faces to the left while the fingers point upward. The finger tips of the right hand are in line with the tip of the nose. This develops concentration. The tips of the fingers of the right hand are in line with the tips of the toes of the right foot. This develops balance. The eyes look forward. The palm of the left hand faces to the right while the fingers touch the wrist of the right arm. There can be no tension. The body is completely relaxed from the top of the head down to the toes. This position can be performed from the opposite side by reversing the above description.

THE BOW STANCE

The body faces the right side. The right leg is forward and bent, but the knee does not go beyond the toes of the right foot. The rear foot is straight. The rear foot holds 40 percent of the body weight while the front foot holds 60 percent of the body weight. The body is held straight. Imagine a straight line running from the back of the head straight down to the base of the spine. The eyes look forward. The right hand rests to the outside of the right thigh. The fingers are relaxed and pointing forward. The left hand is to the center front of the chest with its palm facing forward and its fingers facing up. The elbows of the left arm faces down. There can be no tension. The body is completely relaxed from the top of the head down to the toes. This stance can be performed with the body facing the left side. When this is done the entire description from above must be reversed.

THE HORSE STANCE

The feet are pointing forward and are about two shoulder widths apart. The knees are in line with the toes while the hands are in line with the knees. The hands are held at shoulder level. The right hand fingers hang down and are joined together. The left hand palm points outward with the fingers pointed upward. The shoulders are down. The elbows hang naturally while pointing downward. The spine and head are in line with each other. The two hands symbolize Yin and Yang since they present opposite positions. There can be no tension. The body is completely relaxed from the top of the head down to the toes. The body weight is evenly distributed. This position can be reversed by simply changing the hand configurations.

THE TREADING STANCE

The body is turned to the right. The right leg is bent and the knee is in line with the toes. The left leg is straight. The right leg holds 60 percent of the body weight while the left leg holds 40 percent of the body weight. The body is slightly rounded with the head facing the front. The left hand hangs naturally at the left side with its palm facing the body. The right hand is held up at the middle front of the body. The right hand palm faces to the left while the fingers are pointing up. There can be no tension and the body is completely relaxed.

THE HALF SPLIT LEGS

The body faces to the left. The feet are about two shoulder widths apart. The left foot points to the left while the right foot points forward. The body drops down by bending both knees with the body weight equally distributed. The body is slightly curved forward although there is a straight line from the head to the base of the spine. Both arms are extended forward and are slightly curved. The left palm faces the right while the right palm faces the left. The fingers are pointing forward and the elbows are pointing down. There can be no tension; the body must be completely relaxed. This stance can be performed on the opposite side by reversing the above description.

THE SINGLE FOOT STANCE

All the weight is on the left foot. The left foot is slightly bent while the right leg is raised up with its knee pointing straight up. The right foot is pointing to the diagonal left front. The right arm is raised up with its palm facing forward and it is held slightly above the eyes. The right hand palm is in line with the right knee. The left hand palm is in front of the left leg, pointed down and parallel with the right knee. The back is straight and the arms are rounded. There can be no tension; the body must be completely relaxed.

THE POSTURES OF TAI CHI CH'UAN

1. WU CHI
2. TAI CHI BEGINS
3. THREE POINT CONCENTRATION
4. GRASP THE BIRD'S TAIL
5. SINGLE WHIP
6. STEP UP AND RAISE THE HANDS
7. THE WHITE CRANE SPREADS ITS WINGS
8. BRUSH KNEE AND TWIST STEP LEFT
9. THREE POINT CONCENTRATION
10. REPEAT BRUSH KNEE AND TWIST STEP LEFT
11. BRUSH KNEE AND TWIST STEP RIGHT
12. BRUSH KNEE AND TWIST STEP LEFT
13. THREE POINT CONCENTRATION
14. PLAYING THE FIDDLE
15. STEP UP, WARD OFF AND PUNCH
16. APPARENTLY CLOSING UP
17. CARRY THE TIGER TO THE MOUNTAIN
18. CROSS THE HANDS
19. DIAGONAL BRUSH KNEE AND TWIST STEP LEFT
20. TURN AROUND, BRUSH KNEE AND TWIST STEP RIGHT
21. THREE POINT CONCENTRATION
22. GRASP THE BIRD'S TAIL
23. DIAGONAL SINGLE WHIP
24. FIST UNDER THE ELBOW
25. REPULSE THE MONKEY
26. REPULSE THE MONKEY RIGHT
27. REPULSE THE MONKEY LEFT
28. SLANTED FLYING
29. STEP UP AND RAISE THE HANDS
30. THE WHITE CRANE SPREADS ITS WINGS
31. BRUSH KNEE AND TWIST STEP LEFT
32. NEEDLE AT THE BOTTOM OF THE SEA
33. FAN THROUGH THE BACK
34. TURN THE BODY AND PUNCH
35. RETREAT STEP, WARD OFF AND PUNCH
36. GRASP THE BIRD'S TAIL
37. SINGLE WHIP
38. CLOUD HANDS
39. SINGLE WHIP
40. HIGH PAT ON HORSE LEFT
41. LEG KICKS TO THE RIGHT SIDE
42. HIGH PAT ON HORSE RIGHT
43. LEG KICKS TO THE LEFT SIDE
44. TURN BODY AND KICK WITH HEEL

45. BRUSH KNEE AND TWIST STEP LEFT
46. BRUSH KNEE AND TWIST STEP RIGHT
47. STEP UP AND PUNCH DOWNWARDS
48. TURN AND CHOP OPPONENT WITH FIST
49. STEP UP, HIGH PAT ON HORSE LEFT
50. REPEAT LEG KICKS TO THE RIGHT SIDE
51. RETREAT TO FORM SEVEN STAR POSE
52. RETREAT TO HIT THE TIGER
53. RAISE THE LEG A SECOND TIME
54. DOUBLE FISTS HIT THE EARS
55. TURN THE BODY AND KICK UPWARDS
56. TURN AROUND AND KICK WITH THE HEEL
57. CHOP OPPONENT WITH THE FIST
58. STEP UP, WARD OFF AND PUNCH
59. APPARENTLY CLOSING UP
60. CARRY THE TIGER TO THE MOUNTAIN
61. CROSS THE HANDS
62. DIAGONAL BRUSH KNEE AND TWIST STEP LEFT
63. TURN AROUND, BRUSH KNEE AND TWIST STEP RIGHT
64. THREE POINT CONCENTRATION
65. GRASP THE BIRD'S TAIL
66. DIAGONAL SINGLE WHIP
67. THREE POINT CONCENTRATION
68. WILD HORSE PARTING ITS MANE RIGHT
69. WILD HORSE PARTING ITS MANE LEFT
70. WILD HORSE PARTING ITS MANE RIGHT
71. THREE POINT CONCENTRATION
72. WILD HORSE PARTING ITS MANE RIGHT
73. FAIR LADY WORKS AT THE SHUTTLES LEFT
74. FAIR LADY WORKS AT THE SHUTTLES RIGHT
75. THREE POINT CONCENTRATION
76. WILD HORSE PARTING ITS MANE RIGHT
77. FAIR LADY WORKS AT THE SHUTTLES LEFT
78. FAIR LADY WORKS AT THE SHUTTLES RIGHT
79. THREE POINT CONCENTRATION
80. GRASP THE BIRD'S TAIL
81. SINGLE WHIP
82. CLOUD HANDS
83. SINGLE WHIP
84. CREEP DOWN
85. GOLDEN COCK STANDS ON ONE LEG RIGHT
86. GOLDEN COCK STANDS ON ONE LEG LEFT
87. REPULSE THE MONKEY LEFT
88. REPULSE THE MONKEY RIGHT
89. REPULSE THE MONKEY LEFT
90. DIAGONAL SLANT FLYING
91. HANDS RISE UP
92. THE WHITE CRANE SPREADS ITS WINGS
93. BRUSH KNEE AND TWIST STEP LEFT
94. NEEDLE AT THE BOTTOM OF THE SEA

CHAPTER 3

THE FORMAL EXERCISE OF TAI CHI CH'UAN

Before actually performing Tai Chi Ch'uan the student must reflect upon the basic principles provided in the beginning of this book. Attention must be paid to proper posture and concentration. All breathing is done through the nose in a natural and relaxed manner. As the student becomes proficient in the performance of Tai Chi Ch'uan, the exercise itself will develop the proper method of breathing within the student.

All body movements must be performed slowly and continuously. It is of the utmost importance that the student be completely relaxed. If Tai Chi Ch'uan is not performed in a relaxed manner, then the student is not performing Tai Chi Ch'uan.

Each movement should flow into the next movement. The body is engaged in a continuous process of change until the end of the exercise is reached. At all times, the mind must flow without any obstruction. When you are performing Tai Chi Ch'uan do not think of anything else. Your mind must be focused on the performance of the exercise.

It must be noted that this book is merely a guide for the student. To really learn Tai Chi Ch'uan, a qualified instructor must be sought out.

PRINCIPLES OF BREATHING

1. All breathing is performed through the nose.
2. The tongue touches the roof of the mouth.
3. The entire body is relaxed.
4. All breathing is natural. Do not raise up the shoulders. Do not overexpand the chest.
5. Breathe with the diaphragm.

WU CHI

Stand straight with the knees slightly bent and the arms hanging naturally at the sides. The feet are shoulder width apart. The body is completely relaxed.

TAI CHI BEGINS

Slowly raise both arms to shoulder height. The palms are facing down. Gradually lower the wrists and the elbows, allowing the arms to drop to the sides. The palms are facing forward. As the arms come to rest at the sides of the body, lower the body by bending at the knees. The palms are facing down.

Step forward with the left foot, allowing only the heel to make contact with the ground. All the body weight is on the right foot. The left hand comes forward and raises up, palm facing the body, slightly above the waist. The right hand comes forward and raises up, palm facing outward, to shoulder height. The hands appear as though they are holding a sphere. Gradually turn the left foot to the right side and then let the left foot come in complete contact with the ground. At the same time, the right hand sinks down while the left hand raises up. Shift the body weight to the left foot. Slowly turn the body to face the right side.

THREE POINT CONCENTRATION

Slide the right foot to the left front, letting it rest on its heel. The left hand sinks down while the right hand raises up. The finger tips of the left hand are touching the wrist of the right hand. The tip of the nose is in line with the tips of the fingers of the right hand. The tips of the toes of the right foot are in line with the tips of the fingers of the right hand. The shoulders are relaxed. The elbows point to the ground, which allow the shoulders to be down. The body weight is on the left foot.

GRASP THE BIRD'S TAIL

Draw the palms toward the body. Without stepping, lower the right foot to the ground and transfer 60 percent of the body weight to the right foot with the remaining 40 percent on the left foot. The whole body moves forward and circles from left to right by pivoting from the basal spine, which causes the arms to move in a larger circle. As the circle starts to once again go to the left, sit back, raising the right foot up on its heel. Turn the right heel slightly to the left and then lower the right foot to the ground.

SINGLE WHIP

Push the right palm to the left side. The fingers of the right hand come together and are pointing down. With the left foot, step to the left. The left palm moves from right to left rotating outward so that the palm faces away from the body. The hands are in line with the knees and everything is balanced.

STEP UP AND RAISE THE HANDS

Shift the body weight to the left. The right foot steps forward on its heel. The right and left hands appear to be holding a ball in front of the body. Drop the right foot to the ground and slide the left foot up to the right foot.

The right hand raises up while the left hand drops down. Bend at the waist, keeping the head and neck straight. Turning from the basal spine, circle the body from left to right. The hands do not move. As the body starts to come up, the hands move to the left. The palms are facing down. The hands circle up until they are in front of the body with the palms facing outward.

BRUSH KNEE AND TWIST STEP LEFT

Turn the right foot slightly to the right. Draw the hands to the right rear by the side of the head. The left palm faces outward while the right palm faces inward. The hands appear to be holding a small ball. Step forward on the left heel. Twist the waist slightly to the left and lower the left foot to the ground. The left hand circles down above the left knee with the palm facing the knee. While the left hand circles down, the right hand pushes forward with its palm facing outward.

THREE POINT CONCENTRATION

Repeat the Three Point Concentration that follows the First Brush Knee and Twist Step Left.

The palms circle so that they face each other and then circle to the right rear by the side of the head. The right palm faces inward while the left palm faces outward. The hands appear to be holding a small ball. Lower the left foot to the ground and circle the hands to the right front. The left hand drops down above the left knee while the right hand pushes forward.

BRUSH KNEE AND TWIST STEP RIGHT

Turn the left foot slightly to the left. Draw the hands to the left rear by the side of the head. The left palm faces inward while the right palm faces outward. The hands appear to be holding a small ball. Step forward on the right heel. Twist the waist slightly to the right and lower the right foot to the ground. The right foot has 60 percent of the body weight while the left foot has 40 percent. The right hand circles down above the right knee with the palm facing the knee. While the right hand circles down, the left hand pushes forward with its palm facing outward.

BRUSH KNEE AND TWIST STEP LEFT

The hands move slightly toward the body and then gradually move outward. The hands appear to be holding a small ball. The right hand is on the outside with the right palm facing inward. The left hand is on the inside with the left palm facing outward. Bend the knees slightly and lift up the heels of both feet. Pivot to the left on the balls of the feet. The hands, still holding the small ball, circle to the right front. Lower the right heel to the ground while stepping out with the left foot. The left foot rests on its heel. The body weight remains on the right foot. Lower the left foot to the ground so that 60 percent of the weight is on the left foot and 40 percent of the weight is on the right foot. At the same time, the left hand circles down in front of the body and comes to rest above the knee. As the left hand circles down, the right palm pushes forward. The left palm faces the knee. The movement of the hands follow the turning of the waist from right to left.

THREE POINT CONCENTRATION

Sit back with the weight on the rear foot. The left foot raises up and rests on its heel. Raise the left hand so that the tips of the fingers are in line with the tip of the nose. The tips of the fingers of the left hand are also in line with tips of the toes of the left foot. The palm of the left hand faces to the right. While the left hand is rising up, the right hand pulls back so that its fingers are touching the wrist of the left hand. The palm of the right hand faces to the left.

PLAYING THE FIDDLE

Let the body weight gradually come down on the left foot until the left foot is firmly on the ground. The two palms come together and then circle from right to left. Continue circling the palms for a second time while bringing the right foot to the left foot.

STEP UP, WARD OFF AND PUNCH

Step out with the left foot while letting the hands come forward. Sit back so that the left foot rests on its heel. The left hand is in line with the nose. The right hand makes a fist and pulls back to the waist. Gradually move forward letting the left foot come in complete contact with the ground. The right hand punches out as the body moves forward.

APPARENTLY CLOSING UP

The left palm moves under the right elbow. Sit back by allowing the right leg to bend while the left leg straightens out. The left foot rests on its heel. At the same time that the body sits back, pull both hands to the waist. Both of the palms are facing up. Circle both palms upward and then push outward as the body moves forward. The body moves forward by lowering the left foot to the ground, bending the left leg and straightening the right leg. Both palms are now facing outward.

CARRY THE TIGER TO THE MOUNTAIN

Drop both hands in front of the body. The palms are facing down. Lift up the heel of the front foot and pivot to the right on the ball of the foot. Shift the body weight to the right foot and then pull the left foot to the right foot. The body and the feet should be pointed to the diagonal left. As the left foot slides to the right foot, turn the hands over so that the palms are facing up. Circle both hands outward and upward. The palms and elbows are facing down. The spine is relaxed and straight. The lower half of the body is heavy (positive) while the upper half is light (negative).

CROSS THE HANDS

Bring the arms together so that the hands are crossed. The palms face outwards, the elbows face down and the shoulders are relaxed.

DIAGONAL BRUSH KNEE AND TWIST STEP LEFT

Rotate the palms so that they face each other and then circle the palms to the right rear by the side of the head. The right palm faces inward while the left palm faces outward. The hands appear to be holding a small ball. While the hands are circling to the rear, step out with the left foot letting it rest on its heel. The body is still facing the diagonal left. Lower the left foot to the gound and circle the hands to the right front. The left hand drops down above the left knee while the right hand pushes forward.

TURN AROUND, BRUSH KNEE AND TWIST STEP RIGHT

Rotate the palms so that they face each other and then circle the palms to the left rear by the side of the head. The left palm faces inward while the right palm faces outward. The hands appear to be holding a small ball. Pivoting on the heels of both feet, the body turns 180 degrees to the right so that it faces the left diagonal rear. As the body pivots to the rear, lower the right hand so that it is above the right knee and push forward with the left palm.

THREE POINT CONCENTRATION

Sit back and raise the hands up. The right foot rests on its heel. The position of the body, feet and hands are the same as the Three Point Concentration that follows Tai Chi Begins. The only difference is that this Three Point Concentration faces the diagonal left rear.

GRASP THE BIRD'S TAIL

DIAGONAL SINGLE WHIP

This movement is like the Single Whip, however, it has the following exceptions: 1. It faces the diagonal left front. 2. The fingers of the right hand do not come together. 3. Do not stop the movement in this position. The left foot pivots to the left on its heel.

FIST UNDER THE ELBOW

While turning left on the heel of the left foot, slightly turn to the left on the heel of the right foot. Slide the right foot so that it is to the right rear of the left foot. Let the arms circle to the left so that they are in front of the body. The body is facing the left. Sit back and raise the left foot so that it rests on its heel. Pull the arms back slightly toward the body and let the right hand come to rest under the left elbow. As the right hand comes under the left elbow, both the right and left hands make fists. The fists are held loosely.

REPULSE THE MONKEY

Lower the left foot to the ground and bring the body forward, circling it to the left. As the body circles to the left, open up both fists and pull both hands to the left rear by the side of the head. Both palms are facing each other with the left palm facing inwards while the right palm faces outwards. The hands appear to be holding a small ball. Step back with the left foot while pushing forward with the left palm and lowering the right hand so that it is above the right knee. The palm of the right hand faces the knee.

REPULSE THE MONKEY RIGHT

Sit back and rest the right foot on its heel. Pull the hands back to the right side of the head. The hands appear to be holding a small ball. Step back with the right foot. At the same time, push out with the right palm and lower the left palm so that it is above the left knee.

REPULSE THE MONKEY LEFT

Sit back and rest the left foot on its heel. Pull the hands back to the left side of the head. The hands appear to be holding a small ball. At the same time, push out with the left palm and lower the right palm so that it is above the right knee. As the hands are moving forward, step back with the left foot.

SLANTED FLYING

Turn right on the heel of the right foot. Lower the left hand so that it is about waist high with its palm facing up. Pull back the right hand so that it is about chest high with its palm facing down. The hands appear to be holding a large ball. Step to the left diagonal rear with the left foot. The left hand raises up to shoulder height while the right hand sinks so that it is above the right knee. The hands rise and sink as if they were moving along a slanted board. Shift the body weight to the left foot.

STEP UP AND RAISE THE HANDS

Turn the body slightly to the right by pivoting right on the heels of both feet. The body is now facing the front. Raise up the right hand so that it is about waist high with its palm facing the body. Lower the left hand so that it is about chest high with its palm facing out. Both hands are in front of the body. Slide the left foot forward so that it is even with the right foot.

THE WHITE CRANE SPREADS ITS WINGS

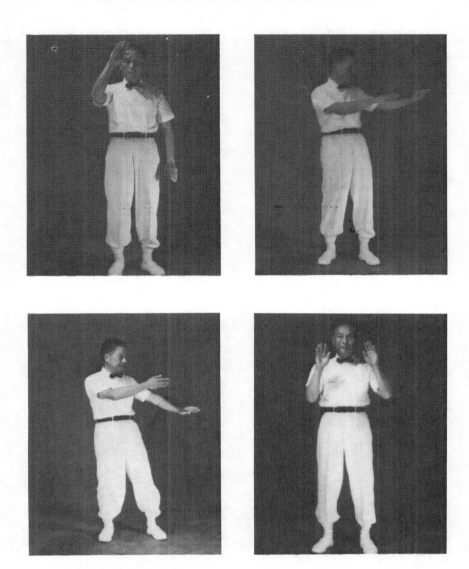

Raise up the right hand, lower the left hand and repeat The White Crane Spreads Its Wings.

BRUSH KNEE AND TWIST STEP LEFT

NEEDLE AT THE BOTTOM OF THE SEA

Take a small step forward with the right foot. Pull back the right hand until it is in line with the left hand. Sit back and pull the left foot up so that it rests on its toes. Raise up the left hand and lower the right hand. The fingers of the left hand point upward while the fingers of the right hand point downwards.

FAN THROUGH THE BACK

The left foot steps forward on its left heel, which straightens the left knee. Lower the left foot to the ground and bring the body forward. Lower the left hand and raise up the right so that they are parallel with palms facing each other. Slowly turn the body to the right by pivoting to the right on both heels. As the body turns to the right, pull back the right hand so that it is to the right side of the head with its palm facing out. The left hand turns over with its palm facing the left and its fingers pointing up. The fingers of the right hand are pointing toward the left hand. The balance is on both feet.

TURN THE BODY AND PUNCH

Let both arms drop down in front of the body. Both palms are facing down. Turn the body to the right by pivoting to the right on the left heel and sliding the right foot to the right. The body is facing the right. The right hand makes a fist and both hands circle up the front of the body and then circle down in front of the body with the palm of the right fist pointing up while the palm of the left hand points to the right. The fingers of the left hand are pointing up. Both hands are about waist high.

RETREAT STEP, WARD OFF AND PUNCH

The left palm covers tne right fist palm. Circle the hands forward moving left to right, allowing the hands to return to their original position. As the hands circle forward, step back with the right foot and raise up the left foot so that it rests on its heel. Circle the hands forward once again, but when they are in front of the body, pull the right fist back to the waist and push the left hand forward. The fingers of the left hand are pointing upward and the palm is facing to the right. Lower the left foot to the ground and punch forward with the right fist.

GRASP THE BIRD'S TAIL

Sit back so that the body weight is on the right foot. The left foot rests on its heel. Open the right fist so that the palm points upward. The fingers of the left hand rest on the wrist of the right hand. The left hand palm points down. Step forward with the right foot and repeat Grasp the Bird's Tail.

SINGLE WHIP

CLOUD HANDS

The left hand circles down and up to the right. The right hand opens up and both palms face each other. As the left hand circles to the right, shift a portion of the body weight to the right foot. The left hand will now circle in front of the body with the palm facing the body. The right hand circles down and to the left with the palm facing the left. As the hands circle to the left, shift the weight to the left foot and slide the right foot over to the left foot. Continue to circle the arms so that they are now moving to the right side. Step to the side with the left foot and repeat the above movements two more times.

SINGLE WHIP

On the final Cloud Hands, when the hands are on the right side with the right palm facing away from the body and the left hand palm is facing up, let the fingers of the right hand come together. Step to the side with the left foot. As the left foot steps to the side, let the left hand circle in front of the body with the palm facing the body. When the left hand passes the left shoulder, turn the hand so the palm faces diagonally left.

HIGH PAT ON HORSE LEFT

Turn the right foot slightly to the right and then turn the body to the left. Shift the weight forward and then backwards. Pull the left foot back and let it rest on its toes. The left hand pulls towards the body with its palm up. The right hand crosses the body with its fingers pointing up and its palm facing left.

LEG KICKS TO THE RIGHT SIDE

Step forward with the left foot. At the same time, the right hand circles upward and to the right while the left hand circles downward and to the left. Both hands form loose fists as they follow a figure eight pattern and come to rest by the left side of the head. The arms are wrist to wrist with the right arm on the outside. Slide the right foot up to the left and pull up the right foot so that it rests on its toes. Turn the left foot and the body slightly to the left. The hands, still holding fists, are crossed in front of the body. Lift up the right leg and slowly straighten out the leg. The kick is from the tips of the toes. The hands spread out with the right hand over the right leg while the left hand extends to the left at shoulder level.

HIGH PAT ON HORSE RIGHT

Drop the right leg to the ground so that it comes to rest on its heel. The leg should be lowered slowly. The right hand drops to the inside front of the body while the left hand drops to the outside front of the body. Lower the right foot to the ground while shifting the body weight forward. The right hand rotates so its palm is facing up while the left hand pulls back with its fingers pointing up and its palm facing to the right.

LEG KICKS TO THE LEFT SIDE

Turn the right foot and body slightly to the right. The left hand circles up and to the left while the right hand circles down and to the right. The hands once again follow the figure eight pattern as they come to rest by the right side of the head. Both hands form loose fists. The left foot slides up to the right foot and rests on its toes. Slowly raise the left leg and let it gradually straighten out. The kick is from the tip of the toes. The arms, which are wrist to wrist with the left arm on the outside, open up. The fists open up with the left hand extending over the left leg while the right hand extends to the right at shoulder level.

TURN BODY AND KICK WITH HEEL

Slowly lower the left leg behind the right leg while crossing the arms, wrist to wrist, in front of the body. The left arm is on the outside. Turn the body to the left rear. Slowly raise the left leg and gradually extend the leg so that it kicks with its heel. Open up the arms with the left arm extending over the left leg while the right arm extends to the right side at shoulder level.

BRUSH KNEE AND TWIST STEP LEFT

Slowly lower the left leg letting it come to rest on its heel. The hands circle to the right side of the head and appear to be holding a small ball. The right palm faces inward while the left palm faces outward. Lower the left foot to the ground. At the same time, the left hand circles down, coming to rest above the left knee while the right palm pushes forward.

BRUSH KNEE AND TWIST STEP RIGHT

STEP UP AND PUNCH DOWNWARDS

Circle the hands back to the right side of the head with the right palm facing inward while the left palm faces outward. Step forward with the left foot. Keeping the head and neck straight, move the body forward. The left hand circles downward, crossing over the left knee, and continues to circle upward and to the right, coming to rest in front of the body with the palms facing to the right. The fingers of the left hand are pointed upward. The right hand makes a fist and punches downward.

Fold the arms in front of the body, placing the right arm on top of the left arm. Pivot to right rear on the heels of both feet. Circle the right foot to the right front. The left hand extends out while the right hand, which has formed a fist, circles forward and pulls back to the waist.

STEP UP, HIGH PAT ON HORSE LEFT

Step forward with the left foot. At the same time, circle the right hand to the rear and then open up the fist while pushing forward with the palm of the right hand. The palm faces the left. Draw the left hand back with the palm facing up and the fingers pointing forward.

REPEAT LEG KICKS TO THE RIGHT SIDE

Since the left foot has already moved forward it is not necessary to repeat this step. The rest of the movement is the same as Leg Kicks To The Right.

RETREAT TO FORM SEVEN STAR POSE

Bring the right foot back to the diagonal left rear. Pull the hands in front of the body with the left palm facing the right side and the right palm facing the left forearm. Switch positions so that the left palm faces the right forearm and the right palm faces the left side. At the same moment that the hand positions switch, step back with the left foot.

RETREAT TO HIT THE TIGER

Drop both hands in front of the right knee. Turn the basal spine to the left rear. The left hand rises up with its palm facing forward. The right hand is in front of the body with its palm facing left.

RAISE THE LEG A SECOND TIME

Turn the body to the right by pivoting on the left heel. The left hand should have the appearance of pouring whiskey while the right hand should have the appearance of a cup. Spread the hands to the side and kick up with the toes of the right foot.

DOUBLE FISTS HIT THE EARS

The right foot comes down on its heel and faces the right diagonal front. The hands circle up and then down, coming to rest in front of the body. Both hands grasp fists and circle forward to hit the opponent's ears. As the fists circle forward, lower the right foot.

TURN THE BODY AND KICK UPWARDS

Turn the body to the right by pivoting from the basal spine. The hands circle downward and cross in front of the body. The right foot pivots to the right side while the left foot steps up on its toes. Kick out with the left foot by letting the toes kick upward. At the same time let the arms spread out.

The left foot steps across the right leg. Turn the body to the right rear by pivoting on the heel of the left foot and the toes of the right foot. The arms are crossed in front of the body as the body starts to turn. When the body has completed its pivot, spread out the arms and kick with the heel of the right foot.

CHOP OPPONENT WITH THE FIST

Lower the right foot on its heel. The right hand, holding a fist, circles toward the body and then, while circling forward, pulls back to the waist. The left hand circles toward the body and then extends forward with the palm facing the right side.

STEP UP, WARD OFF AND PUNCH

The palms of both hands come together in front of the body with the left palm on top. Circle the palms from right to left. As the palms start to circle for a second time, repeat Step Up, Ward Off and Punch.

APPARENTLY CLOSING UP

The left palm moves under the right elbow. Sit back by allowing the right leg to bend while the left leg straightens out. The left foot rests on its heel. At the same time that the body sits back, pull both hands to the waist. Both palms are facing up. Circle both palms upward and then push outward as the body moves forward. The body moves forward by lowering the left foot to the ground, bending the left leg and straightening out the right leg. Both palms are now facing outward.

CARRY THE TIGER TO THE MOUNTAIN

Drop both hands in front of the body. The palms are facing down. Lift up the heel of the front foot and pivot to the right on the ball of the foot. Shift the body weight to the right foot and then pull the left foot to the right foot. The body and the feet should be pointed to the diagonal left. As the left foot slides to the right foot, turn the hands over so that the palms are facing up. Circle both hands outward and upward. The palms and elbows are facing down. The spine is relaxed and straight. The lower half of the body is heavy (positive) while the upper half is light (negative).

CROSS THE HANDS

Bring the arms together so that the hands are crossed. The palms face outwards, the elbows face down and the shoulders are relaxed.

DIAGONAL BRUSH KNEE AND TWIST STEP LEFT

Rotate the palms so that they face each other and then circle the palms to the right rear by the side of the head. The right palm faces inward while the left palm faces outward. The hands appear to be holding a small ball. While the hands are circling to the rear, step out with the left foot letting it rest on its heel. The body is still facing the diagonal left. Lower the left foot to the ground and circle the hands to the right front. The left hand drops down above the left knee while the right hand pushes forward.

TURN AROUND, BRUSH KNEE AND TWIST STEP RIGHT

Rotate the palms so that they face each other and then circle the palms to the left rear by the side of the head. The left palm faces inward while the right palm faces outward. The hands appear to be holding a small ball. Pivoting on the heels of both feet, the body turns 180 degrees to the right so that it faces the left diagonal rear. As the body pivots to the rear, lower the right hand so that it is above the right knee and push forward with the left palm.

THREE POINT CONCENTRATION

Sit back and raise the hands up. The right foot rests on its heel. The position of the body, feet and hands are the same as the Three Point Concentration that follows Tai Chi Begins. The only difference is that this Three Point Concentration faces the diagonal left rear.

GRASP THE BIRD'S TAIL

DIAGONAL SINGLE WHIP

Perform the Single Whip facing the diagonal left.

THREE POINT CONCENTRATION

Turn the body slightly to the right side and slide the right foot to the left so that it is in front of the body. Repeat Three Point Concentration.

WILD HORSE PARTING ITS MANE RIGHT

Draw the right foot back to the left foot. Let the right foot rest on its toes. The right hand drops in front of the body while the left hand is in front of the right shoulder. Step out to the diagonal right on the right heel, and then lower the right foot. Relax the body and lean to the right. The right hand raises up to the diagonal right while the left hand drops to the left side of the body. The eyes look at the left hand.

WILD HORSE PARTING ITS MANE LEFT

Turn the body to the right by pivoting on the heel of the right foot. The left foot comes up on its toes. The body weight is on the right foot. The left hand drops down in front of the body while the right hand crosses the body coming to rest in front of the left shoulder. The left foot steps to the right foot to establish balance. Step out to the diagonal left with the left foot. The left hand raises to the diagonal left while the right hand drops to the right side. The body leans to the left. The eyes look at the right hand.

WILD HORSE PARTING ITS MANE RIGHT

Turn the body to the left by pivoting on the heel of the left foot. The right foot slides to the left and rests on its toes. The right hand drops in front of the body while the left hand crosses the body and comes to rest in front of the right shoulder. Step out to the diagonal right with the right foot and repeat Wild Horse Parting Its Mane Right.

THREE POINT CONCENTRATION

Relax the body. Turn the body to the right and then pull the body to the rear. The right hand drops in front of the body and circles up. The left hand crosses in front of the body while the right foot withdraws to the left foot. The right foot rests on its toes and then steps forward and rests on its heel. The right hand rises up and the body is in the position of Three Point Concentration.

WILD HORSE PARTING ITS MANE RIGHT

FAIR LADY WORKS AT THE SHUTTLES LEFT

The body turns to the right by pivoting from the basal spine. The hands move to the front of the body and appear to be holding a ball. The right palm faces down while the left palm faces up. Slide the left foot to the right foot and rest it on its toes. Step out to the diagonal left with the left foot and let the heel touch the ground first. The hands circle forward with the left palm facing up and the right palm facing down. The fingers of the right hand are touching the wrist of the left hand. The body and arms circle left to right by pivoting from the basal spine. The body sits back and the left foot comes up on its heel as the circle moves to the rear. Continue to circle forward, allowing the left foot to return to the ground. The left hand rises up with its palm facing out and its fingers facing the right. The right palm pushes forward with its fingers pointing up. The right hand is beneath the left hand.

FAIR LADY WORKS AT THE SHUTTLES RIGHT

Turn the body to the right by pivoting on the heel of the left foot. The hands withdraw to hold the Tai Chi sphere in front of the body. The right foot comes up on its heel and slides to the diagonal right. The body continues to turn as the hands open up with the right palm facing up and the left palm facing down. The fingers of the left palm are touching the wrist of the right hand. The body circles right to left. The body sits back with the right foot coming up on its heel. Continue to circle forward, allowing the right foot to return to the ground. The right hand rises up with the palm facing out while the left palm pushes forward.

THREE POINT CONCENTRATION

Slide the right foot to the left front, letting it rest on its heel. Let the body sit back and repeat Three Point Concentration.

WILD HORSE PARTING ITS MANE RIGHT

FAIR LADY WORKS AT THE SHUTTLES LEFT

Turn the body to the right and slide the left foot to the right, letting it rest on its toes. Step out to the diagonal left with the left foot and repeat Fair Lady Works at the Shuttles Left.

FAIR LADY WORKS AT THE SHUTTLES RIGHT

The body turns to the right by pivoting to the right on the heel of the right foot. The hands pull to the front of the body and hold the Tai Chi sphere. As the body continues to circle, step out to the diagonal right with the right foot and repeat Fair Lady Works at the Shuttles Right.

THREE POINT CONCENTRATION

Slide the right foot to the left, letting it rest on its heel. Raise up the hands and let the body sit back. The position of the body, hands, and legs are the same as the original Three Point Concentration.

GRASP THE BIRD'S TAIL

SINGLE WHIP

SINGLE WHIP

CREEP DOWN

Turn the body to the left. The right hand opens up and moves across the body to the left wrist. The right foot takes a slight step to the right as the body weight is shifted to the right foot. By bending the right knee, slowly lower the body. The left leg straightens out as the body drops down. Move the body forward by shifting the weight to the left foot. Let the body come up with the left hand in front of the body at chest level with the palm facing right. The right hand is down with the palm facing left.

GOLDEN COCK STANDS ON ONE LEG RIGHT

Raise up the right leg. The right hand raises up with the palm out while the left hand drops down with the palm down.

GOLDEN COCK STANDS ON ONE LEG LEFT

The right leg drops down. The right hand goes down and moves toward the body while the left hand raises up and moves forward. The left palm faces down and the right palm faces out. Raise up the left leg.

REPULSE THE MONKEY LEFT

Step back with the left foot. The hands pull back to the left side of the head and hold the Tai Chi sphere. The left palm is on the outside and faces the right palm. The right hand drops down over the right knee while the left palm pushes forward.

REPULSE THE MONKEY RIGHT

REPULSE THE MONKEY LEFT

DIAGONAL SLANT FLYING

Turn the body to the right by pivoting on the heel of the right foot. The hands drop down to hold the Tai Chi sphere in front of the body. Step to the diagonal left with the left foot. Open the hands up with the right hand dropping down above the right leg while the left hand raises up to shoulder level. The left palm faces toward the right while the right palm faces down. Shift the majority of the body weight to the left foot.

HANDS RISE UP

Slide the right foot to the front of the body resting it on its heel and raise the hands up to the front of the body. The position of the hands, feet, and the legs are the same as the original Hands Rise Up.

THE WHITE CRANE SPREADS ITS WINGS

BRUSH KNEE AND TWIST STEP LEFT

NEEDLE AT THE BOTTOM OF THE SEA

FAN THROUGH THE BACK

TURN THE BODY AND PUNCH

The left palm covers the right fist palm. Circle the hands forward moving left to right, allowing the hands to return to their original position. As the hands circle forward, step forward with the left foot letting it rest on its heel. Circle the hands forward once again, but when they are in front of the body, pull the right fist back to the waist and push the left hand forward. The fingers of the left hand are pointing upward and the palm is facing to the right. Lower the left foot to the ground and punch forward with the right fist.

GRASP THE BIRD'S TAIL

Repeat the Grasp the Bird's Tail that follows Retreat Step, Ward Off and Punch.

SINGLE WHIP

CLOUD HANDS

HIGH PAT ON HORSE

HIT OPPONENT'S FACE WITH PALM

Step forward, heel first, with the left foot. The right hand goes forward, drops down and then circles back to the left chest. The right palm faces down. At the same time, the left hand draws back and then the palm pushes forward striking the opponent's face. The body and the left palm move forward at the same time.

Turn the body to the right rear by pivoting right on the heel of the left foot. The right foot turns to the right rear. The hands do not move as the body turns. Swing the right foot up allowing it to move in a circle from left to right. The left hand crosses the body to hit the right toes.

BRUSH KNEE AND TWIST STEP RIGHT

Lower the right foot to the ground and repeat Brush Knee and Twist Step Right.

STEP UP AND PUNCH TO THE GROIN

Step forward with the left leg. The right hand makes a fist and rises up to the left palm as the left palm pulls back slightly. The right fist pulls back to the right waist and circles forward to hit the opponent's groin. The left hand brushes the left knee and then circles to the right front letting its fingers touch the right wrist.

GRASP THE BIRD'S TAIL

Repeat the Grasp the Bird's Tail that follows Step Up, Block and Punch.

SINGLE WHIP

CREEP DOWN

STEP UP, SEVEN STAR POSE

Turn the heel of the left foot slightly to the left. Step forward with the right foot so that it rests on its heel. Both hands make a fist. Raise the right fist so that it is to the left front of the left fist.

RETREAT TO RIDE THE TIGER

The right foot steps behind and to the left of the left foot. Turn the body to the right, letting the right fist open up and turn to the right so that the palm faces right. Open up the left fist and then let the fingers come together. The left hand drops to the rear. The left foot comes up on its toes and then is lifted up so that it faces the diagonal right.

TURN AROUND AND HIT OPPONENT'S
FACE WITH THE PALM

Turn the body to the rear by pivoting to the right on the heel of the right foot. Lower the left foot to the ground, letting the heel touch first. As the left foot steps down, the right palm, which is now facing down, moves across the body to the left chest. As the right palm moves across the chest, the fingers of the left hand open. The left palm then pushes forward to hit the opponent's face.

TURN THE BODY, DOUBLE LOTUS SWING

Turn the body to the rear by pivoting to the right on the heel of the left foot. The right foot raises up on its toes and turns slightly to the right. The hands spread out with both palms facing down and then circle to the right.

The hands are now facing the diagonal right. Swing up the right foot so that it travels in a circle that moves from left to right. Both hands move across the body to hit the toes of the right foot. The right foot steps down on its heel and is facing the diagonal right. Lower the right foot to' the ground. The hands face the diagonal left.

BEND THE BOW TO SHOOT THE TIGER

Turn the right foot slightly to the left so that it points forward. Turn the body to the right. The hands drop down and move to the right. As the hands pass the right side of the body they form fists, circle up and punch toward the front of the body. As the hands punch out, the body turns slightly to the left so that it faces forward. The right fist is on top with its palm facing down while the left is on the bottom with its palm facing up.

HIGH PAT ON HORSE

The hands spread outwards. The left foot slides forward, to the left front of the right foot, and rests on its toes. The left hand circles outwards, turns over and pulls to the front of the body with its palm facing up. The right hand circles to the rear and moves to the front of the body with its palm facing the left while its fingers point up. The fingers of the left hand touch the right wrist.

HIT OPPONENT'S FACE WITH THE PALM

TURN AROUND AND CHOP OPPONENT WITH FIST

STEP UP AND HIGH PAT ON HORSE

Relax. Move the body back by bringing the left foot up on its heel. Lower the left foot and step forward with the right foot. Repeat Grasp the Bird's Tail.

SINGLE WHIP

CLOSING THE TAI CHI

Slide the left foot to the right. The feet are shoulder width apart. The right hand opens up and both hands, palms facing down, move in front of the shoulders. Circle both hands toward the body and then let them drop down to the sides. As the hands drop down, the body rises up.

General Principles
Main Objectives
1. To live is to breathe. Coordination of breathing is actually the core; the foundation of Tai Chi Ch'uan utilizes the mind to activate the *Chi,* or breathing. Correct habit of deep breathing down to the navel psychic center is essential. Tai Chi breathing is embryo breathing, unlike ordinary breathing; accomplished only by practicing Tai Chi.
2. The mind or spirit should be concentrated. Attention should be paid to the inner self. A perfect psychic life can be developed through meditation in movement. Discipline is the assertion of self over self.
3. Physiological movements are determined by the mind. The *Chi* should be lowered down to the psychic center and stuck to the spinal cord. With the activation of *Chi,* the body is moved.
4. All bodily movements (arms, waist, sacrum, and the whole body) should be set loose, light, and natural. Do not exert awkward strength.

Particulars
1. The mind holds the commanding position.
2. The *Chi* is similar to flag leading movements.
3. The waist is the axis controlling movements.
4. Inhalation and exhalation should be in alteration and regular. No panting or hastiness.
5. The eyes should gaze at the moving hand or kicking foot.

Stance Particulars
General
1. Rooting in the feet.
2. Stemming from the legs.
3. Directing by the waist.
4. Expressing in the fingers.

Central Trunk
1. Straightening the head.
2. Sacrum in position.
3. Maintaining the central equilibrium.
4. Set yourself in a state of naturalness and tranquility.

Hands
1. Differentiation of Yin and Yang in substantiality and insubstantiality.
2. Include the form of circles according to Tai Chi.
Steps
1. Differentiation of insubstantiality and substantiality.
2. Alteration of advance and retreat.
Trunk
1. Hollowing the chest.
2. Raising the back.
3. Sitting wrists.
4. Stretching out the fingers.
Posture
1. Easily straight in correct Tai Chi posture.
2. Inner comfort, complete relaxation from head to toes.
3. Wholesome and steady, with mind, spirit, and intrinsic energy coordinated introvertedly.
Mind in Tranquility; Body in Relaxation
1. Loosen arms, shoulders, and drop elbows.
2. Loosen hips, sacrum, stomach, and spinal cord.
3. Concentrate on relaxation; relieve all tension internally and externally; regulate breathing; try to maintain zero stillness; try to maintain a rhythm that will synchronize inwardly and outwardly.
Application of Techniques
Neutralizing Energy
1. Attaching energy. When engaging the opponent in a struggle, attach to his movements in order to prevent him getting away. Aim at advancing.
2. Running energy. Applying the principle of nonresistance, aiming at retreating.
Attacking Energy
1. Hold fast. Use both hands to hold fast the opponent's wrist, elbow, shoulder, arm; make him unable to move and make him lose his balance.
2. Feint energy. Make a feint of attacking. When the opponent takes action, borrow his force and let him lose his balance. Then one may attack the opponent easily.

ABOUT THE AUTHOR

T.C. Lee began his study of Tai Chi Ch'uan in 1933 in Canton. After studying Tai Chi Ch'uan for over a year, he returned to his home in Hawaii. He was not satisfied with his initial instruction in Tai Chi Ch'uan and sought out a master that would provide him with a deeper understanding of the art. Unable to find any such instructor in Hawaii, he returned to China. In 1937, he went to Hong Kong to enter the Tai Chi Ch'uan school of Wu Kam Chin. Wu Kam Chin was the son of Wu Chin Yow, the founder of the Wu style of Tai Chi Ch'uan. Mr. Lee studied under both Wu Kam Chin and his son, Wu Kung Chow. Thus, T.C. Lee studied under both the first and second generation students of the Wu style.

Mr. Lee first studied the Yang style of Tai Chi Ch'uan in 1946 in Hawaii. He was not satisfied with his instruction in the Yang style, so he returned to Hong Kong in 1948 for further instruction.

Mr. Lee first began teaching the Wu style of Tai Chi Ch'uan in 1952 at the Chinese Physical Cultural Assocation in Hawaii. He was the first teacher of the Wu style in Hawaii. In 1956, T.C. Lee and Po Wing Chock opened Tai Chi Ch'uan to students of all races.

It has been my privilege to have studied and to continue to study Tai Chi Ch'uan under the expert guidance of Mr. Lee. He has opened up the depths of Tai Chi Ch'uan and explained to me its three dimensions of physical form, philosophical understanding and spiritual enlightenment.

Mr. Lee wishes to pass on his knowledge of forty-seven years to his fellow man. This book is but an introduction to the wonders of Tai Chi Ch'uan.

Dr. Robert Santee